It's fun to draw Pets

Mark Bergin

WINDMILL
BOOKS
New York

Published in 2012 by Windmill Books, LLC
303 Park Avenue South, Suite #1280, New York, NY 10010-3657

Editorial Assistant: Victoria England
U.S. Editor: Jennifer Way

Library of Congress Cataloging-in-Publication Data

Bergin, Mark, 1961-
  Pets / by Mark Bergin.
      p. cm. — (It's fun to draw)
  Includes index.
  ISBN 978-1-61533-597-8 (library binding)
  1. Animals in art—Juvenile literature. 2. Drawing—Technique—Juvenile literature. I. Title.
  NC783.8.P48B48 2012
  743.6—dc23

2011029719

Manufactured in China

CPSIA Compliance Information: Batch #SW2102WM: For Further Information contact Windmill Books, New York, New York at 1-866-478-0556

Contents

Cat

1 Start by drawing the shape for the head.

2 Add an ear, a face, and whiskers.

3 Draw a bean-shaped body.

You Can Do It!
Use a felt-tip pen for the lines. Add color using colored pencils.

4 Add two back legs and a belly shape.

splat-a-Fact
Cats sleep for 16 to 18 hours a day.

5 Draw two front legs and a tail.

Dog

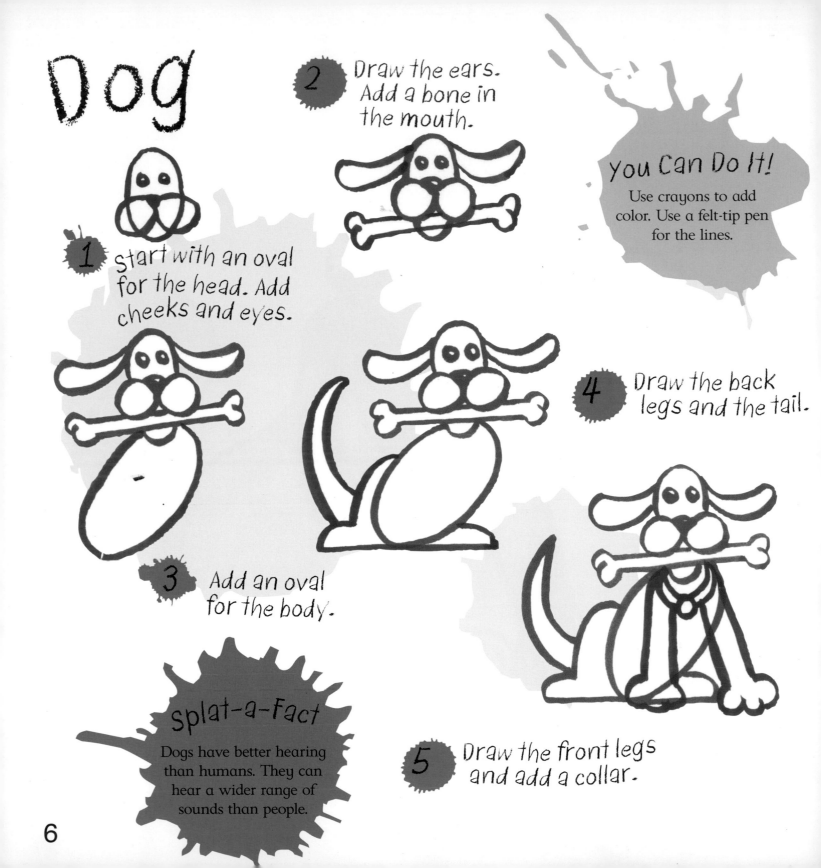

2 Draw the ears. Add a bone in the mouth.

1 Start with an oval for the head. Add cheeks and eyes.

3 Add an oval for the body.

4 Draw the back legs and the tail.

5 Draw the front legs and add a collar.

Splat-a-Fact

Dogs have better hearing than humans. They can hear a wider range of sounds than people.

Fish

1 Start by drawing the body shape.

Splat-a-Fact
Fish sleep with their eyes open!

2 Add a curved line for the face. Draw in the mouth and the eye.

3 Add a tail and two fins.

4 Draw in the stripes.

8

Parakeet

1 Start with the head. Add a beak and a dot for the eye.

2 Add a body and two feet.

3 Draw in the tail feathers.

4 Add the wings.

You Can Do It!

Use oil pastels and smudge them with your finger. Use a felt-tip pen for the lines.

11

Guinea Pig

You Can Do It!
Cut the shapes out of colored paper. Glue them in place. The head overlaps the body. Draw the lines with a felt-tip pen.

1 Start by cutting out a curvy shape for the body. Glue it down.

2 Cut out the head shape. Glue it onto the body.

4 Cut out four feet and brown fur for the guinea pig's back. Stick down.

3 Cut out a brown patch for the face. Glue it down. Cut out and glue down an ear. Draw in the eye and nose.

Splat-a-Fact
A group of guinea pigs is called a herd.

MAKE SURE YOU GET AN ADULT TO HELP YOU WHEN USING SCISSORS!

12

13

Horse

You Can Do It!

Use crayons to create textures. Paint over them with watercolor paints. Use a felt-tip pen for the lines.

1 Start by drawing a bean-shaped body.

2 Draw a neck and a head. Add dots for eyes and nostrils.

3 Draw four legs with hooves.

4 Add a tail and a mane. Draw ears and spots on the body. Add a piece of grass to the mouth.

Splat-a-Fact
Young male horses are called colts. Young female horses are called fillies.

14

15

Lizard

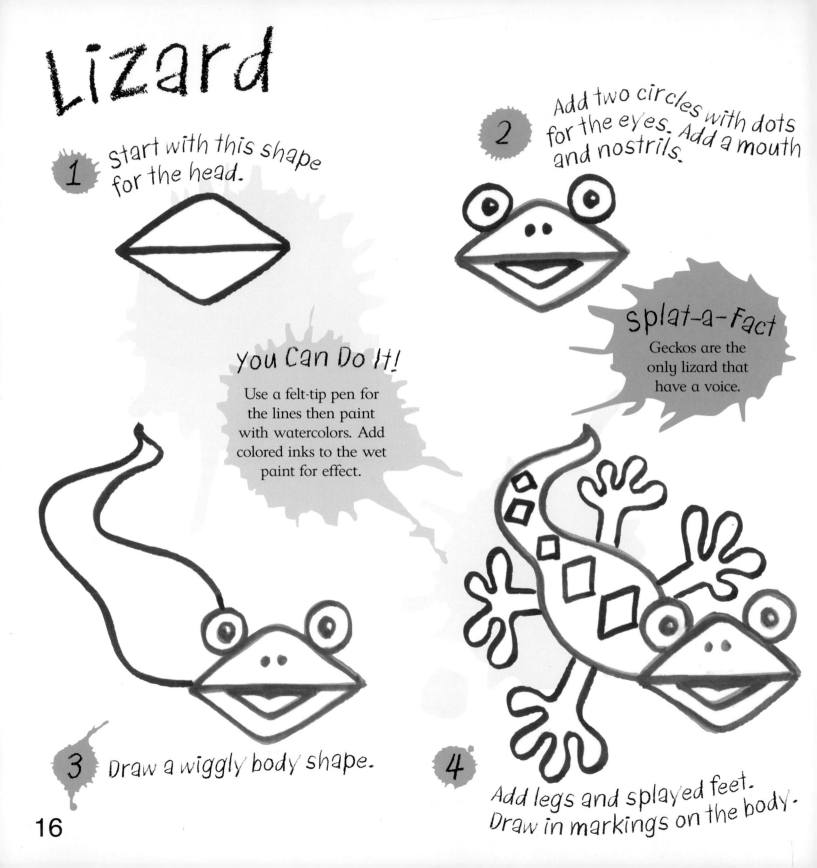

1 Start with this shape for the head.

2 Add two circles with dots for the eyes. Add a mouth and nostrils.

you Can Do It!

Use a felt-tip pen for the lines then paint with watercolors. Add colored inks to the wet paint for effect.

splat-a-Fact

Geckos are the only lizard that have a voice.

3 Draw a wiggly body shape.

4 Add legs and splayed feet. Draw in markings on the body.

16

Parrot

1 Start by drawing the head shape. Add a dot for the eye.

Splat-a-Fact
There are more than 350 different kinds of parrot.

2 Add the body and the beak.

3 Draw the wings and tail feathers.

4 Add the feet and perch.

5 Draw in the feathers.

You Can Do It!
Add color with watercolor paints. Use felt-tip pens for the lines.

Rabbit

1 Start by drawing a circle for the head.

2 Add ears.

3 Draw in the eyes, nose, mouth, teeth, and whiskers.

You Can Do It!
Use oil pastels and smudge them with your finger. Use a felt-tip pen for the lines.

4 Add a rounded body and two back feet.

5 Draw in the front legs and paws.

21

Rat

1 Start with the head shape. Add a dot for the eye.

2 Draw two ears, a nose, a mouth and whiskers.

3 Draw the body.

4 Draw in the two back legs.

5 Draw in the front legs, and a tail. Add toes to each foot.

You Can Do It!
Draw the lines with a felt-tip pen. Add color with watercolor paints.

Snake

1 Start by drawing the head shape.

2 Add dots for the eyes and nostrils.

Splat-a-Fact
Snakes use their forked tongues to smell!

3 Draw in the mouth and add a forked tongue.

4 Draw a long, curving body.

You Can Do It!
Draw the lines with a felt-tip pen. Glue down torn tissue paper for color.

5 Add diamond shapes.

24

Stick Insect

1 Start with the head shape. Add the eyes.

2 Add two antennae. Add pincer shapes under the head.

3 Draw in the stick insect's body.

4 Add three legs and feet to each side.

You Can Do It!
Use crayons to create texture and paint over your drawing with watercolors.

Splat-a-Fact
Stick insect eggs can take 2 years to hatch.

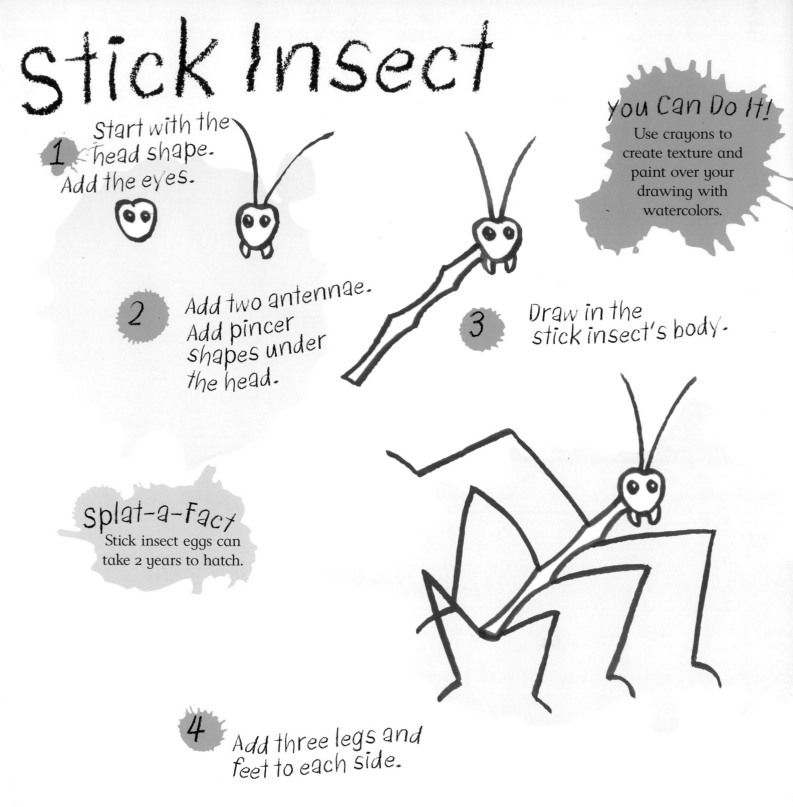

26

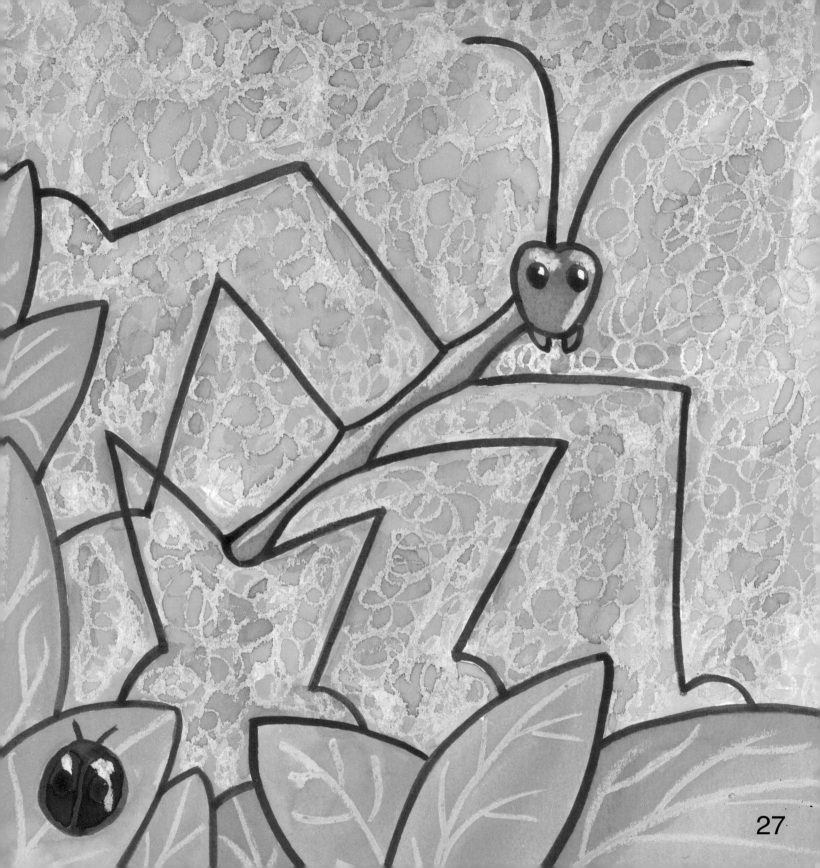

spider

1 Start by drawing two overlapping circles for the head and body.

2 Add four eyes and two fangs.

3 Draw three legs on each side.

4 Add two more front legs.

You Can Do It!
Place textured surfaces under the paper. Then color with crayons to create interesting effects.

28

29

Tortoise

You Can Do It!
Color with watercolor paints. Use a felt-tip pen for lines.

1 Start with an oval shape for the shell.

2 Add pattern to the shell. Draw in another curved line around the shell's base.

3 Draw the head and add an eye, a mouth, and nostrils.

4 Add four legs and a pointed tail.

Splat-a-Fact
Tortoises can live for more than 150 years!

31

Read More

Kennedy, Marge. *Pets at the White House.* New York: Scholastic, 2010

Scheunemann, Pam. *Cool Jobs for Young Pet Lovers: Ways to Make Money Caring for Pets.* Edina, MN: Checkerboard Books, 2010.

Stevens, Kathryn. *Parakeets.* North Mankato, MN: Child's World, 2009.

Glossary

antennae (an-TEH-nee) Thin, rodlike feelers on the heads of certain animals.

nostrils (NOS-trulz) The openings to the nose.

reptile (REP-tyl) A cold-blooded animal with lungs and scales.

smudge (SMUJ) To blend together.

texture (TEKS-chur) When something looks like it has different kinds of surfaces.

whiskers (HWIS-kerz) Hard hairs that grow on a face.

Index

Web Sites

For Web resources related to the subject of this book,
go to: www.windmillbooks.com/weblinks and select this book's title.